SAVE TIME AND MONEY PREPARING FOR DIVORCE

A workbook for those considering divorce or separation

By: Steven B. Chroman P. C.

Copyright © 2012
The Law Office Of Steven B. Chroman P.C.

All rights reserved.

No part of this book may be reproduced in any form or by any electronic or mechanical means including information storage and retrieval systems, without permission in writing from the author. The only exception is by a reviewer, who may quote short excerpts in a review.

Disclaimer:

This workbook is informational only and should not be considered legal advice.

Your attorney is the only one who can and should give you legal advice specifically concerning your case.

"Yes, you will make mistakes. You will think you know best. You will be hurt and angry and mad or sad at the world.

You will face challenges, but you have taken the first step by reading this workbook.

Together we will help you learn, and overcome those challenges, one by one.

Proper preparation will be the key to achieving the best outcome in your case.

This is a guide to help you prepare for your Divorce Planning. It will help you do so with reason and thoughtfulness."

Steven B. Chroman

The Decision No One Wants To Make:

The decision to divorce is never an easy one. There is no doubt you may have many reasons for ending your marriage. Whatever those reasons may be now is not the time for anger, it is more important to control your emotions.

While no one wants to hear it, now is the time for calm, thoughtful, rational planning.

You must focus your attention on what is necessary to get through the divorce successfully. You must think past today and into the future; what it is that you want for yourself and for your children.

This book is a guide to help prepare you for what you must do, especially while you still have ready access to the family home, financial documents, records, and files.

Am I Ready For Divorce:

Elisabeth Kübler-Ross, a pioneer in the hospice movement, first described the stages of recovering from a major trauma such as death or divorce:

• Denial: "This is not happening to me. It's all a misunderstanding. It's just a midlife crisis. We can work it out."

• Anger and resentment: "How can he [she] do this to me? What did I ever do to deserve this? This is not fair!"

• Bargaining: "If you'll stay, I'll change" or "If I agree to do it [money, childrearing, sex, whatever] your way, can we get back together?"

• Depression: "This is really happening, I can't do anything about it, and I don't think I can bear it."

• Acceptance: "Okay, this is how it is, and I'd rather accept it and move on than wallow in the past."

Am I Ready For Divorce Continued:

Understanding these stages can be very helpful when it comes to talking about divorce and decision-making.

It's important to know that when you are in the early stages of this recovery process, it can be challenging to think clearly or to make decisions at all, much less to make them well.

All of a sudden, non-emotional questions arise - for instance: are my bank accounts under both of our names or how about the title to our home and cars?

Have I looked over our will, health and life insurance policies? Do I have accessible cash? Do I have a place to stay if I need to leave?

If the answer to any of these questions is "no," don't panic. Remember, you are still in the decision making and recovery phase.

However, when the time comes, these are issues you will need to be aware of.

Like anything else in life, divorce is a process, it takes time and knowledge. When the time comes, you can be sure you will be more confident with what you took the time to know.

But That's Not Fair:

As a family law attorney, I frequently hear this from people the first time they walk into my office. The first thing I tell them is that people who spend a lot of time worrying about whether or not something is "fair" tend to have difficulties while going through a divorce.

Divorce is a process, governed by laws and precedent.

Determining what's fair and what isn't can be a tough call in many areas of life, in business, in sports, even the grade on your child's last test.

However, nowhere is it more difficult than in the midst of a marriage ending.

If you are going to get divorced or in the midst of a divorce, a very hard, yet realistic fact that clients must face is, decisions in divorces are not based on what you, your soon-to-be ex-spouse, or a judge thinks would be fair.

And in divorce court, arguing about whether something is fair is usually a waste of time and money.

Divorce court decisions are made by applying laws and past case decisions to facts that are presented at your hearings and trials.

The hardest part to deal with sometimes is that all of this is being decided, 'judged' by someone who doesn't even know you.

Despite the above, human decency sometimes triumphs over the odds.

We don't hear about it as much since as a society we focus on the 'entertainment' aspects of Divorce, but there are a sizable share of the people going through divorces who genuinely want to be fair to their soon to be ex.

Now, that being said, everyone involved simply feels best when the judge's decision accomplishes something that seems fair for all and not exaggerated to one party or the other in a divorce proceeding.

But That's Not Fair Continued:

Some people unfamiliar with the judicial system believe that trials are designed for judges to hear evidence and then decide what is fair. But there are two major reasons why they don't work that way: human subjectivity and the reality of the legal system.

The American justice system requires that exactly the same laws and principles must be applied to every case that comes through the courts.

The problem is that often the 'law' can't take into account the complicated human issues that appear in divorce.

In too many instances, the laws simply don't fit into the reality of what is happening in court or for that matter in the lives of those going through a divorce.

The fact remains, if we didn't have laws that all judges applied in deciding each and every case, the judicial system would simply be too unpredictable.

But That's Not Fair Continued:

The positive side of this typically one-size-fits-all approach is that with the laws and precedents available, a seasoned, educated and experienced "family law" attorney knowledgeable in family law and continues to remain updated with recent changes in the law and cases, is able to not only advise with better precision and clarity, a seasoned "family law" attorney can assist their clients with strategy, reasonable settlement alternatives, and cost of their case.

That's a 'fair' way to put it.

How a Pre or Post Nup can help:

Financial trouble is one of the top reason couples divorce today.

With the housing market in the dumps, or just beginning to rebound, unemployment through the roof and the cost of education skyrocketing it's been tough for all of us here in 'the real world.'

When times get tough, marriages get strained.

A prenuptial agreement between Hollywood's rich and famous often makes headlines, but it has a little known friend; the post nup. This lesser known medium can be a great avenue to salvage shaky marriages.

How a Pre or Post Nup can help continued:

What is a post nup? It is any written agreement entered into between spouses after they say, "I do."

Similar to the pre nup, the purpose of postnuptial agreement is to stipulate ownership and division of financial assets in the event a couple divorces.

A couple might seek a post nup for several reasons:

Financial insecurity is undermining the marriage.

You want to provide for dependents from prior marriages.

You didn't define a financial relationship in a pre nup or need to amend your pre nup.

You are considering a temporary separation but not a divorce.

One party's financial circumstances have changed, perhaps through inheritance, promotion, stock options or sale of a business.

You want to specify the division of assets rather than leave it up to the divorce laws of the state possibly saving time, stress and money.

How a Pre or Post Nup can help continued:

Here is a good example I heard of on the news where a post nup saved a marriage.

The news story was about a couple, fighting constantly over money. The husband's business debt had burned through inheritance money, and the couple had a first and second mortgage on their house.

The wife was in fear of being pushed out of her home, while the husband felt his wife didn't have confidence in his business.

A lawyer was able to help them resolve the situation with a postnuptial agreement in which the house was transferred to the wife's name, and the couple agreed to split the mortgage and other household expenses.

The wife no longer feared losing her home, and the husband no longer felt his wife was undermining his business. The fighting stopped.

To quote the wife, "I wanted to divorce his financial problems, not him."

How a Pre or Post Nup can help continued:

Another example where a post nup eased the road to recovery was a couple that had separated, however, was not ready to move forward with a divorce.

Without any agreements in place, one of the spouses feared that their 'share' of the house or estate would not go directly to their children but rather to the other spouse (the children were grown.)

The post nup was a valuable tool to ensure the plan was in place and the couple could focus on what was best for the emotional side of the marriage moving forward, rather than the financial.

These contracts are a way to sort out money problems when, for any number of reasons (inheritances, business failures, business successes, winning the lottery, quitting work), there is more or less of it than there used to be.

It has also become a popular way to deal with the conflicting obligations that arise in blended families.

Think of a post nup as part of an agreement or estate planning, or as a blueprint that was created in calmer times.

Some Things To Think About:

If you are considering getting divorced, you may want to consider going to couple's therapy first.

Often, a good therapist will help you address the core issues that have led to your feelings.

Also, a good therapist will provide you with the right tools for communication.

These tools will be important whether you remain together or ultimately decide to separate or divorce.

If you have children, and end up getting divorced, you will need these tools to communicate with your spouse during and after the divorce.

Some Things To Think About Continued:

During this time while you are considering your future together, you should become aware of your surroundings. In other words, pay attention to the finances.

Are you both balancing the family checkbook?

Are you both paying the credit card debt?

Are bank accounts under both of your names?

Are both of your names on title to your home?

Are both of your names identified with other assets, such as your car?

If the answer to any of these questions is "No," don't panic. However, the financial aspect of your case will be a lot smoother if you are identified with your assets, and you have access to them.

This will all be reviewed in this workbook one by one.

Some Things To Think About Continued:

Additionally, always consider the needs of your children.

Your child is your first responsibility in this matter. Therefore, **if there is abuse of any kind in the household, you should immediately seek out a safe place for yourself and your child**, until a court, with the assistance of your attorney, can address the situation.

Where abuse is not an issue, you should still keep your child's health and happiness at the very top of your list.

The best way to create a healthy environment for your child is to always keep in mind that although you may not love your former spouse, your child does.

Respecting your child's healthy relationship with your ex-spouse will greatly assist your child in adjusting to a very difficult and new situation.

Speaking Of Children…

The Children's Bill of Rights:

I did not write the following 'rights'- I do not take credit for writing these. They are not part of an official document nor do they have any legal basis. I came across them the other day and there was no reference for whom had written them, or I would proudly give them credit. So often in a divorce the parents become wrapped up in their own emotions and thoughts that without meaning to do so, the number one issue can get lost, the children. This is a great written reminder piece that all parents going through a divorce where children are involved, should read just once.

Children's Bill of Rights

We the children of the divorcing parents, in order to form a more perfect union, establish justice, insure domestic tranquility, provide for the common defense, promote the general welfare, and secure the blessings of liberty to ourselves and our posterity, do ordain and establish these Bill Of Rights for all children.

Speaking Of Children…

The Children's Bill of Rights Continued:

The right not to be asked to "choose sides" or be put in a situation where I would have to take sides between my parents.

The right to be treated as a person and not as a pawn, possession or a negotiating chip.

The right to freely and privately communicate with both parents.

The right not to be asked questions by one parent about the other.

The right not to be a messenger.

The right to express my feelings.

The right to adequate visitation with the non-custodial parent which will best serve my needs and wishes.

The right to love and have a relationship with both parents without being made to feel guilty.

The right not to hear either parent say anything bad about the other.

The right to the same educational opportunities and economic support that I would have had if my parents did not divorce.

Speaking Of Children…

The Children's Bill of Rights Continued:

The right to have what is in my best interest protected at all times.

The right to maintain my status as a child and not to take on adult responsibilities for the sake of the parent's well being.

The right to request my parents seek appropriate emotional and social support when needed.

The right to expect consistent parenting at a time when little in my life seems constant or secure.

The right to expect healthy relationship modeling, despite the recent events.

The right to expect the utmost support when taking the time and steps needed to secure a healthy adjustment to the current situation.

Please realize that this is **NOT** law, anywhere.

The "Children's' Bill of Rights" is not legally enforceable, but rather suggestions made to keep the best interest of the child a priority.

Speaking Of Children…

Should A Child Choose Which Parent To Live With:

Sometimes during custody battles or residency decisions parents find themselves involving their children. They do so sometimes hoping the opinion of the child will affect the outcome.

Other times, the children themselves may ask for a change. The child's desire may be influenced by many outside influences; sometimes they might want to be closer to a particular school or friends.

Generally, custody, residency and access decisions are matters for parents to decide.

When parents are unable to reach a decision, they may turn to a counselor for guidance. If that too is unsuccessful, parents may then turn to a mediator and/or lawyer.

Often, the age of twelve is considered a turning point, a time period when the opinion of a child may begin to give added weight to these decisions. However, this number is not set in stone.

Speaking Of Children…

Should A Child Choose Which Parent To Live With

Continued:

The child's maturity, the situation and parental influence will also be important factors.

One must also not forget that the needs of the child and the respective parent's ability to meet those needs in a appropriate and timely fashion are also reviewed.

That said, the decision still remains in the hands of adults, be they the parents, professionals or courts.

Whether child initiated or parent initiated, parents are encouraged to sit down with each other and their older children to discuss openly and sensitively as much as possible.

If in the end parents are unable to resolve matters between themselves, they should consider consulting a counselor, mediator or lawyer to aid in their decision making process.

Just remember, while parents may consult with their older children, one hopes that in the end they will keep the hard decision making process to themselves.

Mediation, Is It The Right Choice For You?

I'm going to save you a couple weeks, months, if not years in answering this frequent question. Take a brief moment to review the essential questions below.

• Have you and your spouse come to a peaceful agreement to end your marriage?

• Has your marriage been free of spouse or child abuse?

*If you have children, are you reasonably certain you and your spouse can reach a peaceful, fair and reasonable agreement regarding child visitation, custody and child support for years to come?

• Are you confident you and your spouse can cooperate to form a fair agreement regarding the division of all your property, retirement funds, assets and payments of debt?

Mediation, Is It The Right Choice For You?

• Do both you and your spouse have access to all financial information including taxes, retirement accounts, debts, and assets in your name, your spouse's name and in both your name?

• Have there been no previous legal proceedings instituted for divorce, legal separation, child custody, or domestic violence between you and your spouse?

If you answer **yes** to **all** of the following questions, then mediation may work for you and your spouse.

If however, any of the answers to the previous questions are no, then there is little doubt you need the experienced aid of an experienced family law attorney.

Financial Picture:

Your first priority will be compiling a complete family financial picture.

Please recognize that the more supporting documentation you can gather, the better.

Never is this more important than if you plan on leaving the marital home.

Make copies of all documents listed below before leaving to spare yourself the possibility of complications, delays, and extra expenses. If there is any potential for domestic violence,

DO NOT put yourself at risk of harm to retrieve records.

Financial Picture:

You will need copies of all of your financial information. Everyone's financial picture is unique, so your records may be quite extensive or may be fairly uncomplicated. You will need to make copies of the following types of documents:

-- Investment accounts (stocks and bonds)

-- Pension and retirement accounts (IRS, 401Ks)

-- Bank and credit union accounts (savings and checking)

-- Credit card accounts

-- Charge card accounts

-- Loans on vehicles

-- Real property mortgages, deeds of trust, or land contracts

-- Insurance policies (beneficiary designations)

-- Pay stubs (make sure you keep all pay stubs)

-- Tax returns for the prior 2 reporting years

-- Business operations records

Financial Planning:

It is always best to go 'overboard' on your documentation history. If possible, retrieve copies all of your records and account information for the past 12-month minimum.

If you are unable to locate certain files or account information to make copies, then at least record the account numbers of those accounts and make a list of the files you could not locate.

Running a credit report of your current status will provide important account details and items you may have overlooked, or forgotten about.

Prepare a realistic budget that reflects what your new living situation may be. If you have children, this will include your child-related expenses.

******Store all of your copies in a secure place.** You may consider opening a safe deposit box, one that is in your name only (not jointly held with your spouse).

Privacy and Security:

If you haven't already, now is the time to **change your passwords** on all financial accounts. You should also change every one of your email account passwords and open a new one for privileged communications with your attorney.

I recommend taking extra precautions, and/or avoidance of Social media such as Face book and Twitter for a time.

To assure your safety, security, and privacy, you should also change the pass code or password on your alarm systems.

Custody Preparation:

If Children are involved, now is the time to begin picturing a 'parenting plan.' This means thinking through everyone's schedules: school schedules and extra-curricular activities, holiday schedules, your work schedule, the other parent's work schedule, doctor visits. Everything will eventually need to be coordinated as part of your proposed parenting plan.

You need to make decisions about who the children will live with. Will there be shared custody? How often will the children be visited by the noncustodial parent?

How are the children's expenses paid for and by whom? Decisions must also be made over the children's healthcare, education, religion, and welfare.

If you do not intend to seek primary physical custody of your children, then you need to make sure you think through what would be your level of involvement so that you can maximize your parenting time.

Your Own Bank Account:

If you don't already have one, then you need to open a new bank account in your name. You may take your half of the marital community's cash and direct deposit that amount into your new account.

If you have direct deposit be sure to inform your payroll department of the new account.

*** Your wages and earnings are still marital property. Earnings remain community property until the petition for dissolution is filed and served, or until you and your spouse enter into a separation agreement.

Review your existing account's current bank statement for any debit or credit accounts that need to be moved to your new account for payments.

If you pay bills by automatic withdrawal or receive automatic deposits from any other source, then you will need to transfer those debit and credit accounts to your new savings or checking account.

Inventory:

This is the time to take inventory of all of your personal property.

If leaving the marital home, or if you have a personal item you don't want to lose, then you should put these items in your new safe deposit box.

Break out that video camera and take photographs or video record all of the community property, as well as the overall condition of the house.

When you go through the marital home, make a list of your personal property as you go from room to room. You will later be able to use this for any insurance purposes as well.

Community property is marital property. In general, community property includes all assets and property accumulated during your marriage, regardless of whether the asset is in one spouse's name or the other.

***Separate property includes any assets that were owned prior to the marriage, or were acquired by gift or inheritance during the marriage.

Your Home:

We know that staying in your home, particularly when children are involved is a very important matter. This requires careful consideration.

***If you want to stay in the marital home during and after the divorce, then don't leave.

This is a new life and a new start. Be sure to consider the condition of the home, the neighborhood, the possibility of selling, and the availability of alternate housing before you commit to staying or leaving the marital residence.

*** If there is a potential for domestic violence then your safety and the safety of your children comes first! Leave the marital home for a safer environment or safe house. If you or your children are threatened with domestic violence, immediately contact your local police or county sheriff.

Choosing The Right Attorney:

Many of us never thought the day would come that we would need to hire an attorney- let alone a divorce attorney…it is a difficult and emotional time, and yet you must make the right decision or you could end up losing a lot of time and money.

I find many of my potential clients are ill informed as to what questions to ask, and after they have 'interviewed' other attorney's they are even more confused than when they began.

I believe we can all benefit by having a little help in the interviewing department…it might help others, and honestly it would help me too- because you will leave feeling confident that you hired the right person to represent you.

What questions should I ask a potential Attorney?

Choosing The Right Attorney Continued:

First, please know, that whomever you meet with, all of your communication is privileged if it is a one on one meeting- and you should be as open and honest as possible.

What experience do you have with this type of case?

What are the possible outcomes? (best and/or worst case scenario)

How will we communicate while the case is on going?

Do you have partners or associates that will be working on the case with you?

What role will I play in the case?

How will you get paid?

Are you comfortable trying to solve this without going to trial?

What is your hourly rate? Do you need an advance retainer? (It is not really necessary to ask this as the attorney will probably tell you- however you can follow this question up with; if the case settles tomorrow is the balance of the retainer refundable?

These might seem like very simple questions; however, in the end it is how you feel after they have answered these questions that will help you decide the right attorney for you.

I want to thank you for taking the time to read through this workbook. I hope you feel better prepared for what lays ahead.

I said it in the beginning; this is not an easy process. In fact, it is the most unspoken harsh reality of today's marriages.

Reading this book says that you are ready to take matters seriously, to educate yourself, to not be taken advantage of- and that will make a huge difference in your case, and ultimately your future.

I wish you the best of luck and strength while you go through this process.

Sincerely,

Steven Chroman

This book is informational only and not to be considered legal advice.

For over 15 years, Steven B. Chroman has been providing outstanding legal services to clients in and around Los Angeles County and the Santa Clarita Valley.

The Law Office of Steven B. Chroman P.C., specializes in the area of family and marital law, divorce, mediation, bundled services, uncontested divorce, legal separation, child/spousal support, modification of orders and paternity, as well as child custody/visitation, property settlements, division of property, domestic violence, enforcement of orders and more.

We maintain a focused practice to ensure personalized attention, meeting the needs of the individual client

Concerns involving a divorce or domestic partnership, custody, visitation and so forth can be overwhelming.

Family law issues are difficult, both emotionally and financially and (it) can be hard to make good legal decisions during these times without proper guidance.

Divorce involves significant emotional conflict and economic uncertainty.

When going through a divorce, you cannot underestimate the value of an experienced divorce attorney; one that can understand, explain and help you prepare for what needs to be done.

We understand the importance of an approach that takes into consideration not only the legal issues, but the needs and concerns of each member of the family, be it a child or even the grandparents.

If you need a referral, as you do not live in the area, please send us an email and we can send you a recommendation.

www.chromanlaw.com

divorceworkshop@hotmail.com

Or Call 661-255-1800

This book is informational only and not to be considered legal advice.

Protect What's Yours

DIVORCE | PRENUP | POSTNUP | SUPPORT | PROPERTY DIVISION

 Law Office of Steven B. Chroman P.C. | Your Experienced, Aggressive Attorney

Call for your complimentary consultation today. 661-255-1800 www.chromanlaw.com